# World Issues

# ANIMAL RIGHTS

### Penny Tripp

## Chrysalis Children's Books

# WORLD ISSUES

**ANIMAL RIGHTS**
**DRUGS**
**EQUAL OPPORTUNITIES**
**GENETIC ENGINEERING**
**GENOCIDE**
**HUMAN RIGHTS**
**POVERTY**
**RACISM**
**REFUGEES**
**TERRORISM**

Produced by Roger Coote Publishing
Gissing's Farm, Fressingfield, Suffolk IP21 5SH, UK

First published in the UK in 2003 by
Chrysalis Children's Books
An imprint of Chrysalis Books Group Plc
The Chrysalis Building, Bramley Road,
London W10 6SP

Paperback edition first published in 2005

Editor: Clare Weaver
Editorial Manager: Joyce Bentley
Designer: Vicky Short
Consultant: John Polley
Picture Researcher: Glass Onion Pictures

ISBN: 1 84138 876 9 (hb)
ISBN: 1 84458 394 5 (pb)

British Library Cataloguing in Publication Data for this book is available from the British Library.

Printed in China
10 9 8 7 6 5 4 3 2 1

Picture Acknowledgements
We wish to thank the following individuals and organizations for their help and assistance, and for supplying material in their collections: Associated Press 5 middle (Alastair Grant); Ecoscene 19 (Angela Hampton), 32 (Angela Hampton); Camera Press 35, 38 (Sussex News Agency); Corbis 6 (Flip Schulke), 22 (Paul Seheult/Eye Ubiquitous); Papilio 11 (Robert Pickett); Photofusion 4 (Christa Stadtler); Popperfoto 3, 14, 17, (Reuters/David Gray), 27 (Reuters), 29, 31, 41, 42 (Reuters/Rose Prouser); Rex Features 18 (Sipa), 20 (Sipa), 24 (Richard Austin), 26 (Reso), 28 (Sipa), 40 (Times Newspapers); RSPCA Picture Library 1 (Andrew Forsyth), 7 (E A Janes), 12 (Mike Lane), 13 (June Hassall), 16 (Colin Carver), 45 (Andrew Forsyth), 46 (Ian Jackson); Still Pictures 15 (Roger de la Harpe), 37 (Mark Edwards); Topham Picturepoint front cover (ImageWorks), 5 top (Photri), 5 bottom (PA), 9 both, 10 (ImageWorks), 21 (ImageWorks), 23 (Polfoto), 25 (Momatiuk Eastcott/ImageWorks), 30 (ImageWorks), 33 (PA), 34 (PA), 36 (Corporation of London/HIP), 39 (Photri), 43 (Photri), 44, 47 (PA). The pictures used in this book do not show the actual people named in the case studies in the text.

# CONTENTS

# Jez's Story

*Jez is 19 years old and works at one of Europe's biggest animal research centres. The centre experiments on over 70 000 animals every year to help companies all over the world develop drugs and other products for human use. Its managing director was beaten up outside his home early in 2001 by animal-rights activists trying to get the facility closed down, and other workers there have also experienced violence.*

'I'VE ALWAYS LOVED animals. Ever since I was little I've had pets. When I was about eight, my sister and I finally managed to persuade our parents that we could look after a pair of mice. They were wicked. We've had rabbits, guinea pigs and cats since then.

I decided very early on that I wanted to work with animals after I left school, and I always wanted to be a vet. I had a Saturday job at a rescue centre looking after horses and ponies that had been mistreated or neglected, and it was amazing seeing them getting healthy and starting to trust humans again.

The animals I look after now are used in experiments to find out if new drugs are safe for humans to use. My friends say I'm mad to get involved in something like that. They think I'm dosing animals up to the eyeballs with poisons to find out what happens to them, but I'm not. All the experiments are carefully controlled, and we don't use animals unless we absolutely have to. There are laws that say lifesaving drugs can't be given to humans until they've been tested on animals to make sure they're safe.

Somebody I work with had their car fire-bombed by the animal-rights people. They were sent letters with razor blades taped into them so that they'd cut their fingers when they opened them. Some of the razor blades even had rat poison on them. My boss has been beaten up.

All we're trying to do is help people. My sister has cystic fibrosis, and one of the drugs we're testing at the moment could really be useful to her. Nobody here wants to hurt animals or take unfair advantage of them, and we look after them well. If I thought they were being cruelly treated I'd be the first one to walk.'

## Different beliefs

Jez represents just one particular viewpoint on the complex issue of animal rights today. People around the world hold very different views on how humans should treat animals.

**ANIMAL EXPERIMENTATION**
*Worldwide, millions of animals are experimented on every year to test the possible effects of drugs and other new products, such as cosmetics and household chemicals, on humans and the environment.*

**ANIMALS COME FIRST**
*Many people believe it's always wrong to experiment on animals. Some try to set them free, and others demonstrate or use violence against people and property in order to get their point across.*

**PEOPLE'S RIGHTS**
*Others believe that, as long as animals are treated with respect, humans have the right to use them for their own benefit – receiving lifesaving hospital treatment, as a result of tests originally carried out on animals, for example.*

# What Are Animal Rights?

*Members of animal-rights groups say that animals have the same right as humans do to live freely. They believe that animals' rights – to be free from slavery and ill-treatment – should be protected by national and international law, just as the rights of humans are.*

**H**UMANITY'S RELATIONSHIP with the other animal species on Earth is a complex one. Many people share their homes and their lives with animals, and since the beginning of time humans have assumed the right to make use of animals for their own benefit.

## Who supports animal rights?

There are people all over the world who believe that animals should have rights.

They say that the Universal Declaration of Human Rights protects humans from being exploited, and animals need the same kind of protection. They maintain that animals have the right not to be used to test drugs and other products designed for use on humans, to be killed for their fur, or hunted for pleasure. They are also against some modern farming methods used to raise livestock for people to eat.

Activists like Martin Luther King Jr struggled for many years to get rights for black Americans that equalled those of their white fellow-citizens.

In the wild, the strongest male wins the right to take charge of his social group and mate with the females in it.

## Human rights

The Universal Declaration of Human Rights was set out by the United Nations in 1948. It says that people everywhere, no matter who they are, are born free and equal. They have basic rights and freedoms that should be protected by national and international law. In return, they have the responsibility to respect the rights and freedoms of others, and to observe the laws and customs of the societies they live in.

Some animal-rights activists use violence against humans and property in order to make their point, while others may set captive animals free. Many follow the ideas of Peter Singer, a philosopher writing in the 1970s, who said it's wrong to regard animals as inferior to humans. He used the word *speciesism* to describe the way humans discriminate against animals, and compared this behaviour to racism.

### Who objects to animal rights?

Some people argue that animals don't need rights. Animals, they say, aren't as intelligent as humans. Only humans can understand ideas like duty and responsibility, and realize that they have to give something back in exchange for the right to live as they choose.

### What other views are there?

Many humans believe it is acceptable to use animals for their own benefit as long as they look after them properly and treat them kindly.

# Who Owns The Animals?

*In prehistoric times, the relationship between humans and other animals was a question of survival: kill or be killed. It was only later that humans realized animal flesh could feed them, and animal hides protect them from the weather. Over thousands of years, humans found many uses for animals and their habitats.*

THE EARLIEST HUMANS only survived by getting rid of, or avoiding, anything that threatened them. Over time they learned that animal flesh was good to eat, and that other foodstuffs produced by animals, such as eggs, milk and honey, also tasted good. They discovered that animal skins could provide them with protection from the cold.

Many land-based animals, as well as those that flew or swam, were hunted and killed by humans for their meat and their skins. Other animals were strong, and could be used to pull heavy things, or frighten enemies, or travel for hundreds of miles without food or water to take valuable goods to those who would pay money for them. Humans thought the Earth and the animals living on it belonged to them.

## Who says humans own the animals?

The Bible says that God made man in His own image, and gave him 'dominion over the fish of the sea, and over the fowl of the air, and over the cattle, and over every creeping thing that creepeth upon the earth'.

It wasn't until the seventeenth century, when a few influential European thinkers raised questions about whether people had the right to treat animals as they did, that anyone gave a thought to the idea that animals might be anything other than human property. When Charles Darwin suggested in the late 1850s that humans were just highly evolved apes, descended over millions

## *DEBATE* - Do animals need rights?

- Yes. Animals need rights because they've been exploited and cruelly treated by humans for millions of years. Humans have taken advantage of them, destroyed their natural habitats, and given them nothing in return.

- No. Animals aren't capable of intelligent thought, or of knowing when they're being unfairly treated. They don't need rights because they are inferior species, put on Earth for the benefit of humans.

In countries where farmers are too poor to afford tractors, or where wheeled vehicles cannot work, animals supply plough-pulling power.

of years from species resembling gorillas and chimpanzees, people began to wonder whether the planet and everything in it really had been created simply for humanity's benefit.

Darwin's theory of evolution, described in his book *The Origin of Species* (1859), argued that for any species to survive and prosper, it had to be the best at dealing with all the challenges life threw at it. He called this 'the survival of the fittest'.

Maybe early humans had just been better than other animals at protecting themselves against predators. Maybe they were just more highly evolved, and able to think about things in a different way. For example, they were able to invent weapons and traps – something other animals have not yet evolved the ability to do. It's not hard to imagine that humans took power over other animals simply because they could.

*Sigourney Weaver as Dian Fossey in the film* Gorillas in the Mist, *the story of Fossey's work with primates in central Africa. Dian Fossey was murdered in 1985, possibly by the poachers who threatened the mountain gorillas she had studied and protected for many years.*

# Are Animals The Same As Humans?

*Once Darwin had suggested that people were simply highly evolved apes, human philosophers, scientists and religious leaders found themselves with questions to answer. Some decided there was no difference between humans and animals, and others were convinced that humans must be superior.*

**W**HEN A PREHISTORIC man successfully hunted down and killed an animal that was going to keep him and his family in food and clothing for months, he wasn't asking whether he had the right to do this. He might, however, have been wondering whether life was always going to be this difficult, and if there were any ways of making it easier.

Over time, humans realized they could feed and house and care for animals conveniently near to where they lived, and kill them when they were ready to, rather than only when they could be caught. These people started the first farms. They found out that some animals made willing workers, too, and were much less trouble than human ones. Some were quite fun, and good to have around, almost like part of the family.

## Are animals inferior to humans?

René Descartes, a French scientist working in the seventeenth century, was one of the first to experiment on animals to see how similar they were to humans. When he cut them open and they

*Few people now share Descartes' view that cutting open an animal is no different from sawing a piece of wood.*

Research has shown that primate behaviour is similar in many ways to that of humans.

screamed, he said that the noise they made was simply a mechanical one. It was no different from the screech of a saw blade on metal. He didn't believe animals could experience either pain or pleasure. The idea that they might have intelligence or emotions just didn't enter his thoughts.

Even today, some people think that animals are inferior to humans and are just another natural resource to be used for mankind's benefit. Modern observation and research has left others in no doubt that animals experience happiness, sadness, fear, pain, anger and boredom, just as humans do. They question whether people can continue to treat animals as they have done in the past now that they know so much more about them.

Many people, however – maybe influenced by animal-rights campaigners, or their own experience of living or working with animals – recognize that animals may not be machines, but that they are still not quite human. They think it should be possible to use animals for the benefit of humanity without mistreating them, and that people should try to find ways of doing this.

## Animal intelligence

Dr Steve Best is an Associate Professor at the University of Texas in El Paso. He uses the achievements of animals like those listed below to illustrate his belief that humans are not the only intelligent species living on Earth.

● Koko the gorilla has a sign-language vocabulary of 500 words and does Internet chats.
● Alex the parrot knows the names of over 100 different objects, seven colours and five shapes. He can count objects up to six, and speaks in meaningful sentences.
● Another gorilla, called Michael, loved opera singer Luciano Pavarotti so much that he wouldn't go outside when Pavarotti was on television.
● Hoku the dolphin grieved when his companion, Kiko, died.
● A chimp called Flint died of a broken heart when his mother, Flo, died.

*Source: Dr Steve Best,*
*www.utminers.utep.edu/best*

## Are animals intelligent?

Animals don't necessarily have to learn the same things that humans know in order to be called intelligent.

By the middle of the twentieth century, scientists were trying to find out how animals, including humans, learned things. Their results showed that many animal species altered their behaviour in order to deal with changing conditions. Rats, for example, could learn how to get to the middle of a maze to find food. This ability to adapt behaviour according to circumstances made it clear that some animals are indeed intelligent.

## Do animals have feelings?

Research has shown that, just like humans, animals feel happy when things go their way, and sad or angry when they don't. If they are doing what they want, in the company of those they want to be with and in pleasant surroundings, they experience happiness. If they are deprived of their freedom or made to suffer in some way, they feel sadness, fear, pain, anger and boredom.

*Many creatures have worked out how to use tools to make their lives easier. A song thrush smashes a snail's shell against a stone to get at its next meal.*

Unhappy animals make their feelings plain. They whine, pace up and down, injure themselves, stop eating, or lash out at their neighbours. Swans, who mate for life, pine if their partner dies. A captive animal in a too-small cage will bang its head against the bars, pull its fur out, or simply sit and rock backwards and forwards.

Caged animals may show many signs of distress and unhappiness.

## *DEBATE* - Are animals sentient (feeling) beings?

- Yes. Animals think, feel and suffer just like humans. Maybe they can't speak like people do, or write things down, but they can still experience the same kinds of emotions.
- No. It's nonsense to claim that animals experience things like humans do. Giving animals names and treating them like humans is inappropriate. We make the mistake of thinking that their responses are emotions like ours.

# What Is Humanity's Relationship With Animals?

*The relationship between people and animals has always been based on the idea that human interests are more important than those of animals. People hunt animals for food, clothing and sport, and use the land animals live on for their own purposes.*

MOST PEOPLE IN today's world no longer hunt animals in order to protect themselves or to survive, although some still have to. Wild animals are now hunted for many reasons: for food, for their furs or skins, to keep their numbers down, and sometimes purely for the fun of it.

### Why hunt animals for food or fur?

Some animals are now specially bred and farmed for humans to eat, while others still thrive better in the wild. Their meat is highly prized because it's more difficult to get, and so can be sold for high prices. People in some parts of the world make a living from hunting or trapping animals that can't be farmed, and selling their meat or fur.

Some people hunt wild animals because they wouldn't have meat to eat, or clothes to wear, if they didn't.

### Why hunt animals to keep numbers down?

If too many animals share the same living space, both the animals and their environment can suffer. Animals have to compete with each other for food, and large numbers can mean there isn't enough to go round.

Many wild animals are themselves food for others, and their numbers are controlled by predators (animals that hunt and kill them). Some species have no natural predators and are culled (hunted and killed) by humans.

*Hunting foxes with dogs is part of traditional country life in the UK, though increasing numbers of people think it's cruel and unnecessary.*

# Why hunt animals for fun?

People hunt animals for sport all over the world. They enjoy the challenge of tracking down and killing their prey. Sometimes they eat what they kill. Sometimes the size of what they catch is the important thing, or the number of animals caught. In the USA, large mammals like deer and bear are targets. In the UK, game birds like partridge, pheasant and quail are all specially reared and hunted for sport. Game birds aren't farmed in the same way that chickens are. They are protected while they breed so they can be shot for food only at certain times of the year. In other European countries, wild birds like larks and thrushes are hunted. Freshwater and sea-dwelling fish like salmon and tuna are hunted for sport, and for the table, all over the world.

Some species of wild animals have been brought to the point of extinction by over-hunting, or have had their habitats destroyed because of the way people use the land.

*People used to go on safari to kill wild animals for sport. They took home tusks, horns, antlers or skins as trophies. Now, they take photographs and videos as souvenirs.*

*Some mink released by animal-rights activists from fur farms in the UK have turned feral (wild) and prey on both farmed and wild animals.*

## Why are animals farmed?

Although some wild creatures – tuna, whales and seals, for example – are still hunted for food, other animals have been farmed since humans realized it was easier to keep them nearby and under control. Cattle, sheep and goats have been domesticated so that their meat, milk and skins would be readily available. While sheep, and other animals kept for their valuable wool, do not have to die so humans can use what they produce, other animals do.

Even some people who recognize that there are good reasons why animals are farmed for food find it hard to accept that they should be kept and killed for other purposes.

## Are animals farmed just for food?

Some wild animals, such as mink, are kept confined on fur farms so that their skins can be made into clothes and other luxury goods. In the wild, mink have large territories and roam freely. Kept in cages, they show many signs of stress. They are killed when they are around seven months old, when their winter coat is fully developed. The killing methods – lethal injection, electrocution or gassing – are chosen so as not to damage their valuable skins.

There are fewer fur farms in the UK than there used to be (the 1995 figure was 13), but they are still widespread in Holland, Scandinavia, Russia and Canada. As well as mink, these farms raise and kill foxes, racoons and wild cats for their fur.

# China's bear farms

While attitudes to the treatment of wild animals are changing in many countries, in others they are not.

'In a tiny iron cage, too small to allow him to stand up or lie down, a young Asiatic black bear is huddled in agony. His stomach is permanently oozing thick, yellow bile from an open wound. Twice a day, a metal tube will be forcibly inserted through the wound into his gall bladder and he will be systematically "milked" of his bile, which will be used in traditional Chinese medicine, cosmetics and even wine. . . In hundreds of bear farms across China, thousands of bears are kept in such conditions. Often taken from the wild, the best they can hope for is a swift death from the pain and shock of the initial operation to open their gall bladder. If they are unfortunate enough to survive, then they are condemned to between five and ten years of torment before their bile dries up and they are simply abandoned...'

*Source: The World Society for the Protection of Animals www.wspa.org*

*Sheep are sheared every year so that humans can take their wool, but other animals have to be killed first and then skinned before their coats can be used.*

# How Are Animals Raised For Food?

*Most people in the Western world buy their food. They no longer have the desire, the space, the time, or the knowledge to raise animals for meat, eggs and dairy products, so they rely on farmers to do it for them. Price is an important issue. People have learned to expect cheap food.*

JUST AS CAR-MAKERS in the early twentieth century realized that they could manufacture and sell their goods cheaply if they produced enough of them and sold them at the right price, so did farmers. Factory farming began in the 1920s when scientists discovered that if certain vitamins were added to animal feed, the animals didn't need sunlight and exercise in order to grow. Farmers could rear large numbers of animals indoors, all year round, and combat any resulting diseases with newly discovered antibiotic medicines.

## How are chickens farmed?

Chickens kept outdoors scratch at the ground, perch, dust-bathe and make nests. Nearly 90 per cent of laying hens –

Factory-farmed chickens raised for their meat are kept indoors, thousands to each shed, and are fed a special diet so that they put on weight quickly.

*Free-range poultry are allowed to scratch and peck outside. They take longer to grow to full size, and their meat and eggs cost more to buy.*

## People and meat

● The average American consumes nearly twice his or her weight in meat each year.

● People share the Earth's natural resources with nearly 1 billion pigs, 1.3 billion cows, 1.8 billion sheep and goats, and 13.5 billion chickens – over two chickens for each man, woman and child on the planet.

● People in the USA, China, Brazil and the European Union eat over 60 per cent of the world's beef, over 70 per cent of the world's poultry, and over 80 per cent of the world's pork.

● China produces and consumes half the world's pork – 85 million tons of it.

● 36 per cent of the world's grain goes to feed livestock and poultry.

● In the USA, farmed animals produce 130 times more waste products than humans.

● Research suggests that people who consume a plant-based diet rich in whole grains, vegetables and fruits are healthier than those whose diet is based on meat.

*Source: www.worldwatch.org*

30 million in the UK alone – are reared indoors in small cages. In the UK over 750 million chickens every year are raised indoors for their meat. They are specially bred so they grow quickly. Crowded conditions can lead to bone deformities and lameness before they are slaughtered at six weeks old.

## How is pig-meat produced?

In the UK, most pigs are housed indoors in groups, though an increasing number are now kept outside. Many pregnant sows give birth in a special crate, and they are unable to make a nest for their piglets or turn around. Young pigs may be fattened in crowded conditions in semi-darkness.

## How are cattle raised?

Many intensively farmed milk-producing cattle spend much of their time indoors. In order to produce milk, they must have given birth to a calf. Their calves are taken away soon after birth, and the mothers are milked by machines. Dairy cattle are bred specially for their milk-producing ability, and may have udders (the part of their body where their milk collects) so big that they find it difficult to walk.

Beef cattle breeds are selected for their ability to turn the food they eat into meat quickly and efficiently, and they may be given special hormones to make them grow more quickly. In some European countries where veal is a delicacy, milk-fed calves are kept in small crates and slaughtered when very young.

## How are fish farmed?

Wild salmon and trout live in open water. Farmed fish are raised in cages or pens suspended in lakes, lochs or coastal waters, before they are killed for sale. Other marine creatures, shellfish such as oysters and mussels, for example, are also farmed.

## How does intensive farming affect animals?

Farmers have learned how to regulate animals' breeding cycles so that eggs are laid, or new animals born, at convenient times.

Animals living under natural conditions – where the number of daylight hours, for example, varies with the time of year – eat and sleep and breed at certain times. Animals kept indoors are exposed to artificial daylight, and produce eggs or young more often than they would naturally.

*Wild salmon travel many miles between their breeding grounds and open water, often leaping spectacularly as they travel upstream to mate. Farmed salmon are kept in cages.*

Intensively farmed milk-producing cattle are specially bred, separated from their calves, fed on concentrates and milked by machines.

Many intensively farmed animals live in man-made spaces designed for easy cleaning and waste disposal, rather than for their comfort.

Animals kept in confined spaces may turn on each other, or on themselves, because they are kept in unnaturally tight spaces that cause them stress. Poultry may have to have their beaks trimmed so they can't cause damage by pecking. Horned cattle routinely have their horns removed. Some chickens actually become deformed because they don't have enough space to grow properly, and others may be crushed or trampled to death.

Diseases and parasites spread quickly through animal communities kept in enclosed spaces. They may have to be treated with powerful antibiotics that can remain in their meat after they are killed.

## *DEBATE* - Does it matter how farmed animals are kept?

- Yes. Animals shouldn't suffer just so humans can eat them. People wouldn't mind paying a bit more for food if it meant animals were better treated.
- No. Everybody has a right to affordable food. Farmers have a duty to provide food at low prices, and it doesn't matter how they do it.

## The rules of religious slaughter

### Hinduism
• Many Hindus are vegetarians because they believe that harming any living thing is wrong.

### Islam
• Muslims may only eat halal meat, which must come from animals slaughtered in a particular way.
• Prayers must be said during the slaughter of an animal.
• Animals must be conscious while the blood is drained from their bodies.

### Judaism
• Jews must eat only kosher meat, which must come from animals slaughtered according to Jewish rules by a qualified butcher.
• The animal's blood must be allowed to drain from its body through a slit in its throat.

### Sikhism
• Sikhs who eat meat will do so only if it is *jhatka*, which means it comes from an animal that has been killed with a single stroke. They cannot eat halal meat.

*Meat hangs in a halal butcher's shop in Brunei.*

## How are food animals killed?

In the UK, more than 2 million chickens are slaughtered every working day. The annual total for sheep and lambs is 19 million; for pigs, 14 million; and for cattle the figure is 3.3 million.

Generally speaking, animals bred for food are no longer slaughtered by the farmers who raised them. Some are transported hundreds of miles to abattoirs (slaughterhouses) to be killed under conditions that are laid down by law. Legislation covers things like animal welfare during the journey to the abattoir, and the slaughtering methods themselves. British law says that animals must be stunned before they're killed, but some religious codes say that animals must be fully conscious when they die. Muslims can follow their own rules, if slaughter takes place in licensed facilities and by licensed slaughtermen.

Millions of chickens are slaughtered, plucked and gutted every day in poultry-processing factories.

## How are animals stunned?

Most sheep and pigs are stunned by having an electric current passed through their brain. Cattle and some sheep are stunned by having a bolt fired from a special pistol into their brain at very high speed. Their throats are then cut so that they bleed to death.

## How are chickens slaughtered?

Poultry slaughter is highly mechanized. The birds are hung upside-down by their legs from shackles attached to a moving line, a bit like a conveyor belt. The line drags the birds' heads through a stunning bath filled with electrified water. Once stunned, or sometimes killed, the moving line then takes them on to automatic neck-cutters. Turkeys are killed in a similar way, except that their necks are cut by hand.

Research has shown that animals can be stressed when they are unloaded from the vehicles taking them for slaughter, by rough handling, and by the unfamiliar noise and smells that surround them. If they aren't properly stunned, they may be conscious and feel pain when they are actually killed.

*The UK government ordered that millions of cattle, pigs and sheep be killed and their bodies burned to try and stop the world's worst outbreak of foot-and-mouth disease in 2001. The disease probably started when infected meat imports were fed to pigs.*

## Why use intensive farming?

The world's human population is growing rapidly and needs to be fed. Farms are becoming bigger and more efficient. Machinery is replacing human and animal labour. New drugs mean that diseases that might once have wiped out large numbers of livestock can be controlled. Farmers can buy new kinds of animal feed based on concentrated nutrients, and supplement their animals' diet with hormones to make them grow faster.

All over the world, intensive farming is now supplying affordable meat. In countries where there are more people than the land can easily support using traditional farming methods, intensive farming may offer a way of reducing malnutrition and starvation. It might not mean happy animals, but it does result in the production of cheap and plentiful food for humans.

## What are the advantages?

Animals can be selected and bred for their ability to produce low-cost, high-quality food for humans. Meat and dairy products are now available all year round, rather than only at certain times.

Intensive farming methods mean that the same amount of land can be made to produce more food, and a greater variety of it. People have more choice about what to buy and eat.

Because supermarkets buy huge quantities of meat and dairy products, they can demand that farmers produce high-quality foodstuffs that are then sold at a relatively low cost.

Research shows that, for many people, price is the most important factor when it comes to choosing food. Foodstuffs produced by intensive farming methods are cheaper than those that aren't.

## What's the human cost?

Fewer and larger farms, and the use of machines rather than human labour, mean fewer agricultural jobs. Many small 'traditional' farmers, unable to compete with their giant neighbours for a share of the market, have gone out of business or are in serious financial trouble.

Food safety has become a big issue. It has been shown that some life-threatening animal diseases may be passed on to humans who eat their meat, and some people think that modern farming methods are partly to blame.

*In many countries, small farms can no longer produce food cheaply enough to stay in business. Suicide rates among farmers are on the increase.*

*Even in a wealthy country, such as the USA, 36 million people are hungry – yet many Americans eat about twice their own weight in meat every year.*

## What's the alternative?

More and more people are becoming unhappy about the way their food is produced. They worry that the drugs and hormones fed to animals will end up in their own bodies when they eat meat, eggs or dairy products.

Animal-welfare organizations all over the world have drawn attention to the way livestock is treated on intensive farms. They say that animals are being treated like machines, and kept in unnatural and unhealthy conditions that cause them severe distress. Other people point out

that most of us aren't exactly starving, and that our farmers are supplying far more food than we actually need.

Many supermarkets and other food suppliers are now offering people a choice. They can either buy cheap mass-produced food, or pay more for something else. Eggs from battery-housed chickens, confined in cages, cost less than eggs produced by chickens kept indoors on straw. These in turn are cheaper than free-range eggs, laid by hens that can run about outside.

Animals, including poultry, that are raised on land that hasn't been treated by pesticides, fed on a 'natural' diet that doesn't include antibiotics and growth-promoters, given room to roam freely, and slaughtered in a way that doesn't cause them pain, are said to be farmed organically. Rearing animals this way costs more, but it is thought to be kinder to them. Sales of organically farmed produce are rising in developed countries.

## Who decides how animals are farmed?

Supermarkets and other retailers (where most people get their food) have enormous influence on what farmers produce. They can refuse to accept meat that has too much fat on it, or is the wrong colour or shape. What they buy from farmers depends on what their customers say they want, and how much they are prepared to pay.

Governments want to make sure that their citizens have enough to eat. They offer farmers money to produce more of certain things, or pay them to use their land in other ways. The media (newspapers, magazines, television and radio) influence what happens by reporting on current events. They also give publicity to groups and individuals trying to change the way people think.

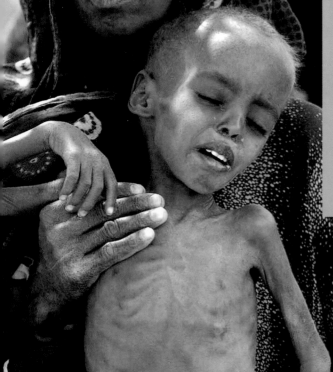

People all over the world, like this child in Ethiopia, are dying because they cannot get enough to eat.

### *DEBATE* - Is human welfare more important than animal welfare?

- Yes. Millions of humans are starving. They need to be fed, and it doesn't matter how their food is produced. Human survival is the most important thing.

- No. Animals don't have to be treated cruelly just so people can eat. People can survive quite easily without them. They can stop eating animal products altogether, or only buy them from suppliers who treat animals kindly.

# How Do We Use Animals For Entertainment?

*Humans all over the world are entertained by animals. They visit zoos and circuses where animals are on show, and attend sporting events where animals are the star performers. Popular films and television programmes feature both wild and domesticated animals, and many people keep animals as pets.*

FOR MANY YEARS, the only chance most people got to see wild animals was when they went to the zoo. Those were the days before television and film brought animals into people's homes almost on a daily basis.

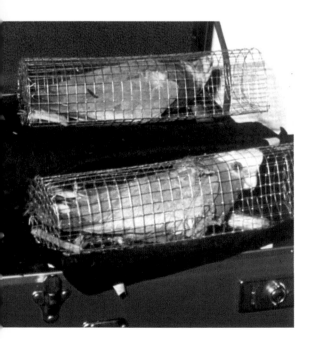

*Many exotic creatures, such as these parrots, are flown thousands of miles from their natural habitats to become household pets. Not all survive the journey.*

Zoo visitors used to find examples of mammals, birds, amphibians and reptiles kept in cages of varying sizes and almost close enough to touch. Protests about the conditions under which the animals were kept became common in the second half of the twentieth century. Things began to change as people realized how far the cages were from the animals' natural habitats.

Today's zoos, including safari and farm parks, are much more likely to keep many of their animals uncaged and out in the open. Some run conservation programmes and breeding projects to help build up the numbers of endangered species. Certain animals, like the giant panda, however, are famous for their determination not to let humans interfere with their sex lives, and will not breed to order.

## How are circus animals treated?

Circus visits are a popular form of entertainment in many parts of the world. As well as clowns, jugglers, fire-eaters and acrobats, people can see elephants, primates, dogs, horses and lions obeying the commands of their trainers and performing all kinds of tricks.

In many countries, animal-welfare campaigners have drawn attention to the way circus and other performing animals are treated. They point out that they are often kept in cramped conditions, and made to learn behaviour that isn't natural for them. Sometimes their training involves punishment for getting things wrong. Some high-profile court cases in the later years of the twentieth century saw circus owners convicted of cruelty, and today's travelling circuses are likely to feature few, if any, animals.

However, performing animals, such as bears, for example, are still highly prized in some parts of the world, and they provide a valuable source of income for their owners.

## What about pet animals?

Many people want animals as pets or companions, and there are breeders and importers who make money by supplying this demand. Some animals are taken from the wild, while others are specially bred.

*Performing animals like this bear photographed in 1963 were once a common sight in circus rings.*

## How are animals involved in sport?

Horse-racing is now a worldwide industry worth millions. Fortunes are made, and lost, by the owners, breeders and trainers of some of the most valuable animals in the world. These horses have their mates carefully chosen for them by humans so that their offspring will, they hope, win some of the huge cash prizes on offer, and go on to produce future winners themselves. Even people who do not deal with the actual horses, such as those working in betting shops, make money from the sport.

Other animals raced for human sport include dogs and camels. Specially bred pigeons are released miles away from where they live to see which can get home quickest.

Some sports, like cock-fighting and dog-fighting, have been outlawed because the aim is for one animal to kill its opponent. Others that involve the likely death of an animal, like bullfighting in Spain and South America, are legal in their countries of origin, but disapproved of elsewhere.

## Why keep companion animals?

Many people have pets. Most are of the cute, furry variety – cats, dogs, rabbits, hamsters, guinea pigs – but snakes, spiders, birds and fish share some humans' homes. Some people think that children who have pets grow up better able to take responsibility for creatures other than themselves, while others keep them simply for the pleasure and company they provide. Some researchers claim that stroking a cat or dog can help a person lower their stress levels; others claim that people living alone have longer, healthier lives if they share their home with a pet.

*Most family pets are well treated and loved, but some may be neglected or abused, and have to be found a new home.*

Matador Finito de Cordoba shows off his bullfighting skills.

## Bullfighting in Spain

• The bull comes into a specially built arena to be greeted by a cape-waving bullfighter – the matador – for a fight that lasts around 15 minutes.

• A fighting bull charges instantly at anything that moves because of its natural instinct and centuries of special breeding. The matador must either kill it, or be killed.

• Picadors first weaken the bull by stabbing it from horseback. Banderillos then approach the bull on foot to attack its shoulders with barbed sticks and make it lower its head so the matador can kill it.

• The matador uses his cape to attract the bull's attention, getting closer and closer to its horns in order to excite the crowd. By now the bull is aware that its life is in danger and, though weakened by the picadors and banderillos, is still dangerous and could kill the matador with one swipe of his horns.

• The matador kills the bull by stabbing it between the shoulder blades, leaping over its horns as he does so.

# Why Use Animals In Research?

*The brain structures of humans and chimpanzees are nearly the same. Many scientific studies have identified the similarities. Humans now understand a lot about their own behaviour as a result of tests done on animals, and regularly use drugs and other products that animal tests have shown to be safe.*

HUMANS HAVE SHARED their world with other animals for millions of years, but it is only in the last few centuries that they have really realized how much can be learnt from them.

The early explorers who left their own countries in search of valuable goods, or who wanted simply to find out what was 'out there', brought back tales of extraordinary creatures their fellow citizens had never seen and could hardly believe. The first rhinoceros brought to London had people running for cover.

The idea that these species were anything other than curiosities lasted for a long time. When scientists suggested other animals might actually have a lot in common with humans, people were aghast.

*Drugs used by vets to prevent and treat animal illnesses are tested on other animals first, to make sure they are safe.*

Some cosmetics carry a label that says they haven't been tested on animals, but others don't.

## Why are other animals so interesting?

It's now known that humans are not the only animals to live in social groups and build complex organized societies. Humans may not be able to understand other species' languages, but research has shown that many animals do communicate with their own kind – warn them of danger, express affection, show each other where the food is.

Some animals are very like humans. When Darwin suggested in the late nineteenth century that mankind was descended from apes, there was uproar. Most people now agree that his ideas make sense, but some still object to them. Researchers continue to study animals to find out how they and their communities work – sometimes in search of knowledge for its own sake, sometimes to see if there are any lessons humans can learn from them.

## What can we learn from animals?

Some animals' brains and bodies are so like humans' that scientists believe that what works for them will work for people, too. If an animal's body reacts badly to something it comes into contact with, the chances are that a person's will as well. If they remain fit and healthy, so will humans. Animals have been used to test whether products like shampoo, eye make-up, washing powder, shower gel and toothpaste are safe for humans to use.

## Does research harm the animals it uses?

If observed sensitively, animals in the wild hardly notice researchers are there. The researchers want to see what animals do naturally, not to interfere and change things.

Other research methods are different. New products like cosmetics and shampoo are often tested on animals to see if they are safe. They may be dropped into animals' eyes or rubbed into their skin. The number of animals that are used in this kind of research is now falling.

Scientists who want to find out what happens when new medicines are given to human patients are required by law to test them on animals first. Some powerful anti-cancer drugs that cause unpleasant side effects in human patients were tested on animals before they were ever given to people.

Scientists now know that pigs' bodies are very similar to humans'. Medical researchers have discovered that organs transplanted into humans from pigs are less likely to be rejected than those from other animals. Specially treated pigskin makes a superb temporary bandage on human burns because it prevents infection and allows the patient's damaged skin to repair itself. Scientists haven't yet worked out a way of getting hold of a pig's heart, kidney or skin that doesn't inconvenience the pig.

## Why make new animals?

New animal parts – or, in a few rare cases, a complete animal – can now be made by means of a process called cloning. Some people believe that cloning will lead to great medical advances for humans. If a human's heart doesn't work properly, perhaps a spare one could be cloned for them out of one of their own cells, or created,

*Dolly the Sheep was the world's first cloned animal, created in 1996 from one of her mother's cells rather than from a fertilized egg. She developed arthritis – usually a disease of the elderly – while still very young, and she died in February 2003 from a lung disease. Scientists are now trying to find out whether Dolly died young (sheep usually live to be 11 or 12 years old) because she was cloned.*

## Organ transplants from animals: examining the possibilities

• There have been about 30 experimental xenotransplants since the turn of the twenty–first century.
• Baboons and pigs are the best xenotransplant donors.
• Baboons are genetically close to humans but carry some dangerous viruses and are in shorter supply than pigs.
• A pig's body is strikingly similar to a human's. Pigs are generally healthier than primates and extremely easy to breed, producing a whole litter of piglets at a time rather than a single offspring as a baboon does.
• Moral objections to killing pigs are fewer since they're already slaughtered for food.

*Source: Rebecca D. Williams, writing on the US Government's Food & Drug Administration's website www.fda.gov*

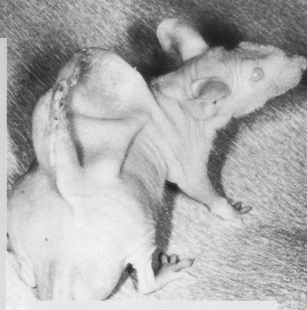

*US doctor Charles Vacanti grew a human ear on a mouse's back in 1995, using the mouse's blood to feed the developing tissue. He believes that other human organs – such as kidneys and livers – could be grown from tiny tissue samples and used to replace diseased ones.*

using another animal's tissue, for transplantation into them.

Maybe animal organs, such as livers or kidneys, could be injected with human genes, so that the body of a person receiving one of them in a transplant wouldn't reject it. Xenotransplants (animal-to-human transplants) could one day be a way of treating patients who now have to wait until a suitable human organ becomes available.

## *DEBATE* - Should animal organs be transplanted into humans?

• Yes. They're easier to come by than human ones and can be genetically altered so the patient's body doesn't reject them. Thousands of human lives could be saved every year.

• No. Animals carry many known viruses, and maybe some that haven't been discovered yet. They could be introduced to the human population by xenotransplants, and prove deadly.

# What Are The Alternatives To Using Animals?

*Over the last fifty years or so, growing numbers of people have decided that humans shouldn't treat animals as they used to. There are ways of living and working that either avoid using animals for the benefit of humans, or use them with greater respect.*

VEGETARIANS CHOOSE NOT to eat meat, and get the protein they need from plant-based sources. Vegans don't eat or use any animal products: they don't eat meat, milk or eggs, and don't wear leather or wool.

Some vegetarians and vegans choose this lifestyle because they don't want to support current food-production methods, or they are concerned that animal diseases and the drugs given to cure them may remain in meat and be

In the UK and other industrialized countries, horse power is no longer used to transport heavy goods over long distances.

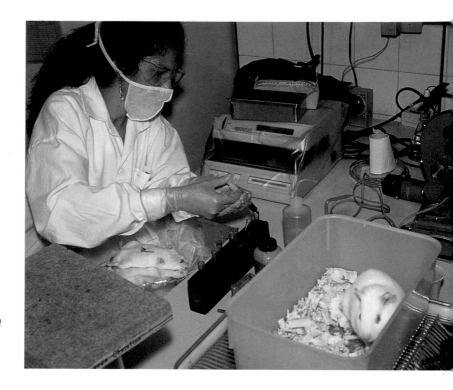

*Chagas Disease is a form of sleeping sickness found only in the Americas, and specially bred rodents are used to research its cause and possible cure.*

harmful to the humans who eat it. Others live this way because they don't believe that humans have the right to eat their fellow creatures.

Leather and fur can now be replaced by man-made substitutes, and animal products once used in the manufacture of household goods, such as soap and cosmetics, have been replaced by chemical substitutes that don't involve animals at all.

## How can animal power be replaced?

Modern industrialized countries rarely use working animals to provide the power to drive machines. Power comes from other sources, such as gas, oil, electricity, water and wind. Any working animals that remain in use are protected from mistreatment by law.

## Can animals in sport be protected?

Many countries now have laws designed to protect animals used in sport and entertainment. Sports like badger-baiting and dog-fighting are banned in many places, and if people are caught participating in them they can be imprisoned. Animal-welfare pressure groups continue to raise awareness of cruel practices both at home and abroad in the hope that they can be stopped. Many people nowadays get their pets from animal-rescue centres, instead of breeders or importers.

## Are animals necessary for testing?

In 1959, British scientists W.M.S. Russell and R.I. Burch published *The Principles of Humane Experimental Techniques*. They suggested that researchers should follow the 'Three Rs': *refine* tests so animal pain or distress is minimized, *reduce* the numbers of animals used, and try to *replace* animals by other methods of testing whenever they could. The number of animals used in product testing has fallen steadily since the 1970s.

*Rescue centres care for wild or domesticated animals that are sick, neglected or abused. They either release animals back into the wild or try to find them good homes.*

## Rescue animal or pet shop pet?

Many animals sold in pet shops have been specially bred for sale, and are products just like chocolate or breakfast cereal. Sometimes, they're kept in cramped conditions and not looked after properly. The people who buy them aren't checked out to make sure they can offer a proper home, and organizations such as the UK's Royal Society for the Prevention of Cruelty to Animals (RSPCA) may be called in to rescue pets that have been abandoned or mistreated – like Salt and Pepper. Salt and Pepper, two adult male cats, were taken to a rescue centre after being abandoned in a dumped car. They were in a cardboard box barely big enough for one cat, and had spent about five days without food or water. They were petrified of people, and tried to attack anyone who came near them. Careful training and lots of patience by the rescue centre staff meant that they could eventually be found new homes.

## How can people avoid using animals?

More and more people are realizing that they can make a difference by making small changes to the way they live.

**What shall I eat?** Some people choose to eat meat and other foodstuffs that come from organically farmed animals that are humanely slaughtered. Others choose not to eat meat or other animal products at all.

**What shall I buy?** People can choose not to buy clothes, shoes, bags and other goods that are made from animal skins. They can buy cosmetics and household goods that haven't been tested in ways that involve cruelty to animals.

**What shall I do for entertainment?** People can choose not to go to circuses and zoos that keep animals in confined spaces or force them to behave in ways that aren't natural to them. They can stop supporting sporting events that endanger animals in some way. There are plenty of alternative forms of entertainment, such as football matches, bowling and the cinema, which don't involve animals.

**Can I avoid drugs tested on animals?** People who eat sensibly and get plenty of exercise tend to stay healthier than those who don't. They may be less likely to suffer from infections that need treatment with drugs tested on animals. Some medical practitioners offer treatments that help patients to avoid using drugs at all.

*People in the twenty-first century can choose not to wear, eat or do anything that harms animals. There are plenty of alternatives.*

# Animal Rights Today

*The animal-rights movement is made up of many groups of people scattered throughout the world. They don't all believe in exactly the same things or use the same tactics to influence people, but they all use newspapers, television, radio and the Internet to publicize their beliefs and get laws changed.*

**A**NIMAL-RIGHTS CAMPAIGNERS use the media because it's an effective way of getting their ideas across to large numbers of people. They hope that, if enough people agree with them, politicians will be forced to make laws that safeguard animals' rights and punish those who break them.

## How do campaigners use the media?

**News** Some hardline animal-rights activists believe that they have to take the law into their own hands to stop humans keeping animals in captivity or using them in any way. They release captive animals into the wild, violently attack people and property, and organize

*Animal-rights campaigners may try to disrupt the events they hate in order to make the news headlines.*

LIVELIHOOD MARCH

28,025 NOW BEEN COUNTED

THANKYOU

BAN MEAT IMPORTS NOT HUNTING!

E & S HUNT

SAVE OUR COUNTRYSIDE

SHOOTING TIMES

BANG OUT OF ORDER

CONSERVATIVE EU

Supported by thousands, peaceful demonstrations make the headlines and show governments how people feel about issues. This is the Liberty and Livelihood March in London, September 2002. Over 400 000 people marched in support of the preservation of rural communities and their traditional way of life.

protests. They do these things to attract the attention of the media, make the headlines, and bring their beliefs to the notice of a wide audience.

Some people argue that the media encourage extremists by reporting on the damage to people and property caused by their actions. They say that if protests and violent attacks weren't publicized, they'd stop.

**Features** Anyone with a point to make can forge relationships with writers and broadcasters, influence what they think and, through them, bring their cause to people's attention. Animal-rights activists, as well as those concerned about animal welfare, keep the media informed about what they believe in, what they are doing, and what they think needs to be done to change things.

**Advertizing** Animal-rights groups and animal-welfare organizations use the media to advertize what they do, and ask people to support them. Printed adverts and broadcast commercials have to conform to certain guidelines, but they can appear in the media as long as they do. And, of course, as long as somebody pays for them!

**The Internet** Many animal-rights campaigners, as well as those who are concerned about animal welfare, have websites on the Internet. They use them to tell people about their current campaigns, recruit supporters, ask for financial support and other help, and influence people's ideas.

Of course, those who oppose the idea of animal rights can use the media to get their point across, too.

### *DEBATE* - Should animals have legal rights?

- Yes. It's the only way we can stop humans exploiting and abusing them.

- No. Animals aren't just differently-shaped, dumb humans. It's ridiculous to suggest they need legal rights. Besides, a human's rights come as part of a package that includes duties and responsibilities. Animals don't have duties and responsibilities.

## Does the law protect animals?

Although there are laws in many countries that define how humans can treat animals, animals still don't have legal rights in the same way that humans do. In 2002, the German parliament became the first in the world to vote that the right of animals to live free from exploitation should become part of the country's constitution.

In 1822, Britain became the first country to make a law covering the welfare of animals, and followed it up with others protecting domestic,

Animal-rights groups use celebrities to help them get publicity. In 1999, Sir Paul McCartney honoured Pamela Anderson Lee for her part in an anti-fur campaign at a gala organized in the USA by People for the Ethical Treatment of Animals (PETA).

The International Whaling Commission (IWC) used to govern how whales were hunted and killed. Now it's more concerned with protecting the survival of the world's largest mammals.

farmed and captive animals. It is an offence in the UK to cause unnecessary suffering to any domestic or captive animal. Those found guilty can be imprisoned for up to six months, fined £5000, or both. Among many other laws are those covering the treatment of performing animals, pets, wild mammals, and working dogs.

The USA has an Animal Welfare Act, as do many other countries. Governments worldwide have joined forces to support the Bonn Convention, which aims to conserve land-based, marine and flying migratory species.

The International Whaling Commission (IWC) controls the extent to which whales can be killed for food and other products. Other organizations also protect other wild species. But, as the World Society for the Protection of Animals (WSPA) points out, 'there is still no government-level international forum at which animal welfare concerns are discussed and ruled upon', let alone one that considers the issue of their legal rights.

In some parts of the world, humans depend on animals for survival.

## *DEBATE* - Are animal rights a luxury in today's world?

- Yes. The survival of the human race is at risk from climate change, population growth, natural disasters and disease. Animal rights aren't as important as finding ways of dealing with these issues.
- No. Animals have the same right to survival as humans do. To argue that one species is more important than another misses the point that all are dependent on each other.

## Are views the same everywhere?

People's attitudes towards animals vary from country to country, and depend on all sorts of things, especially wealth.

Many people today do not directly work on the land or with animals, but in some countries people's chances of survival depend entirely on what they can grow or raise themselves. They may be too busy simply struggling to stay alive to worry about animals. It is only those people who have enough money that can tell lawmakers to protect animals and the land they live on from exploitation. A developing country's need to feed its starving

people may mean it adopts intensive farming methods that use land and water more efficiently than traditional ones.

People in the USA, Canada, Australia, New Zealand, Europe or South Africa can choose to use products like shampoo, washing powder, air fresheners and toilet cleaners that say they aren't tested on animals, but people in other countries may not have that choice. They may not have access to those products at all. A child in

Africa, given life-saving drugs to deal with malaria or AIDS, is probably not aware that they've been tested on animals and probably doesn't care.

## Animal rights or animal welfare?

Some people who have no wish to see animals mistreated or exploited by humans say animals should only be used for human benefit if they are properly cared for. They believe it should be possible to farm animals and slaughter them for food in ways that don't cause suffering. Laboratory animals used to test new products can be looked after well, and not exposed to unnecessary pain. The welfare of animals kept for the purposes of sport, entertainment and companionship can be protected by law.

Animal-rights campaigners say that people who support the right of humans to use animals for their own benefit are missing the point. They compare them with those people who used to regard other humans as their property, keeping them as slaves.

*A friendly, intelligent dog is good company. Should he have the same rights as his owner?*

# I'm only one person. What can I do?

Societies are made up of individual people. Individuals all have the right to their own opinions, and the right to express them. They have the right to influence other people, as long as they do it within the law.

Whatever you think about animals and their rights, you can make a difference. You can find out as much as you can about the way animals are treated, by reading books, newspapers and magazines (see page 51 for some ideas), and by visiting websites like the ones mentioned on pages 52–3.

Everyone can make up their own minds about what they think once they know the facts. Anyone can make lifestyle choices like those on pages 38–9. If you decide that you're concerned about the way animals are treated, you can try to influence your family and friends to think as you do and to make the same kind of lifestyle choices as you have, but

Animals and people often seem to have a special bond; this girl is helping at a donkey sanctuary.

Members of the World Wildlife Fund (WWF) celebrated 40 years of the WWF in 2002, and raised money for panda conservation in China.

remember that they all have the right to make up their own minds, just like you do!

Everyone has the right to join organizations and pressure groups that use legal means to change public opinion and influence the politicians who make laws. You'll find the names and contact details of some influential organizations on pages 52–3.

Anyone can support the work of their chosen organizations by giving money or time to help them do it. They can help organize or support fund-raising events, or give things they no longer need to charity shops that can make money by selling them.

Some people are good at writing letters to local newspapers about the work of

animal charities and rescue centres in their area. Their letters or stories may be interesting enough to be printed, and then other people might be influenced to get involved.

Anyone who thinks animals in their neighbourhood are being neglected or mistreated in some way can let someone know about it, rather than standing back and doing nothing. The kind of person who can help might be a parent or teacher who can talk you through what you know and help you decide what to do next. If they agree that you're right to be concerned, you could contact a local animal charity or rescue centre that can investigate further.

You'll find more suggestions about how to make a difference on the websites of the organizations listed on pages 52–3.

# REFERENCE

## ANIMAL FARMING IN ASIA, AFRICA AND EUROPE

• The greatest concentrations of livestock are in India, China and Europe – where there are most people.

• China farms half of the world's pigs and poultry (most poultry in China are ducks rather than chickens), and their numbers are increasing fast.

• India is the world's biggest milk producer, but the industrialized countries are the most efficient.

• Farmers in India and China can now produce milk, mutton and pork almost as efficiently as the industrialized countries can.

• Livestock numbers are generally increasing worldwide, particularly those of pigs and chickens.

• Some livestock numbers are falling, for example:
    • pigs in parts of Europe
    • bovines (cattle) in most of Europe
    • poultry in Scandinavia and eastern Europe
    • sheep and goats in central Europe and the former USSR.

• Falling numbers don't necessarily mean that less meat is being produced. Production methods are becoming more efficient.

• There are more sheep and goats than cattle in regions north of the tropics, in a band stretching from Spain and Libya to China. Goats are usually more common than sheep near the Equator.

• The developing countries are most efficient at producing meat and milk from sheep and goats.

• Across the world, there is a move away from traditionally farmed ruminant species (bovines, sheep and goats) towards more intensively reared monogastric species (chickens and pigs).

• Ruminant species remain widespread in many of the less-developed regions and continue to be critically important to the rural poor.

• 'Domestic farm animals are crucial for food and agriculture… Around two billion people – one-third of the global population – depend at least partly on farm animals for their livelihoods. Meat, milk and egg production will need to more than double over the next 20 years to feed the growing world population.' (FAO press release, 5 December 2000)

*Source: Animal Health and Production Division of the United Nations' Food and Agriculture Organization  www.ergodd.zoo.ox.ac.uk*

# MEDICAL ADVANCES

• Animal research has helped to develop vaccines, antibiotics and the anaesthetics used in all forms of surgery.

• Without animal research there would have been no organ transplants, blood transfusions, replacement heart valves or kidney dialysis.

• Medicines tested on, or produced from animals can now overcome serious human conditions such as diabetes, asthma and high blood pressure.

• Human illnesses such as cancer, heart disease, depression and HIV are being treated by medicines tested on animals.

• Researchers are using animals to find treatments for conditions such as cystic fibrosis, Alzheimer's disease, stroke, spinal-cord damage and malaria.

*Source: Research Defence Society*
*www.rds-online.org.uk*

---

## ANIMAL WELFARE

• Nearly 200 animal-welfare organizations from 64 countries have signed up to the Universal Declaration for the Welfare of Animals.

*Source: World Society for the Protection of Animals*
*www.wspa-international.org*

## ANIMALS IN LABORATORY EXPERIMENTS

• In the UK, the Netherlands, Germany and several other European countries the number of animals used in laboratory experiments has halved since the 1970s.

• In Canada, mammals have largely been replaced by fish in experiments.

• In the USA, between 18 and 22 million animals a year are used in research.

*Source: Ohio Scientific Education and Research Association  www.osera.org*

# CRUELTY TO ANIMALS, 2001

In 2001, the Royal Society for the Prevention of Cruelty to Animals (RSPCA) in the UK:
• responded to 1 509 317 phone calls (one every 20 seconds).

• received over 123 000 complaints of cruelty.

• rescued or picked up over 195 000 animals.

• brought 1977 cases of cruelty or neglect to court, and secured almost 2500 convictions – nearly 90 per cent of which were for neglect.

Their current campaigns include improving conditions for:
• 38 000 animals used in the EU every year to test new cosmetic ingredients and products.

• 4000 dogs and 1000 monkeys used in UK laboratory experiments every year.

• 820 million chickens raised in the UK for their meat.

*Source: RSPCA www.rspca.org.uk*

# FURTHER INFORMATION

## BOOKS

### NON-FICTION

*Animal Liberation*
by Peter Singer (Pimlico, 1995)
Reissue of Singer's mid-1970s classic, demanding a re-think of mankind's relationship with animals. Not an easy read, but crucial.

*Born Free Trilogy*
by Joy Adamson (Pan, 2000)
Lions in Africa. Made a huge impact and helped open people's eyes to conservation issues.

*Gorillas in the Mist*
by Dian Fossey (Phoenix, 2001)
Fossey was murdered in 1985, maybe by the poachers who threatened the primates she loved and protected in central Africa.

*In the Shadow of Man*
by Jane Goodall (Phoenix, 1999)
Goodall's account of her field study and adventures with chimpanzees in Tanzania.

*Talking with Animals*
by Charlotte Uhlenbroek (Hodder & Stoughton, 2002)
Tie-in with BBC TV series exploring animal communication.

### FICTION

*Animal Farm*
by George Orwell (Penguin, 2000)
Reissue of this classic animals-take-over-the-farm story.

*Black Beauty*
by Anna Sewell (Penguin Books, 1995)
Fine horse goes down in life, and suffers. First published in 1877 and instrumental in getting the use of the cruel bridle outlawed.

*Tarka the Otter*
by Henry Williamson (Puffin, 1995)
Life in the wild through an otter's eyes.

*The Butterfly Lion*
by Michael Morpurgo (Collins, 1996)
A young boy rescues a white lion from the African bush.

*The Old Man and the Sea*
by Ernest Hemingway (Arrow, 1994)
Stunning story of an old fisherman's battle with his last big fish.

*Watership Down*
by Richard Adams (Puffin, 1973)
Rabbits set out to find a new warren. Authentic account of animal behaviour inside a gripping story – as much about freedom and human nature as it is about rabbits.

# ORGANIZATIONS

Many animal-rights organizations produce written information that they will send to you or your school/college if you contact them. Some provide speakers who will talk to young people about the work they do.

## UK
### Animal Aid
The Old Chapel, Bradford Street, Tonbridge, Kent TN9 1AW
Website: www.animalaid.org.uk

### Blue Cross
Shilton Road, Burford, Oxon OX18 4PF
Website: www.bluecross.org.uk

### Compassion in World Farming
Charles House, 5a Charles Street, Petersfield, Hants
Website: www.ciwf.co.uk

### Fight Against Animal Cruelty in Europe
29 Shakespeare Street, Southport, Merseyside PR8 5AB
Website: www.faace.co.uk

### Fund for the Replacement of Animals in Medical Experiments
96–98 North Sherwood House, Nottingham NG1 4EE
Website: www.frame.org.uk

### Research Defence Society
58 Great Marlborough Street, London W1F 7JY
Website: www.rds-online.org.uk

### RSPCA
Wilberforce Way, Southwater, Horsham, West Sussex RH13 9RS
Website: www.rspca.org.uk

### The Vegetarian Society
Parkdale, Dunham Road, Altrincham, Cheshire WA14 4QG
Website: www.vegsoc.org

### World Society for the Protection of Animals (WSPA)
89 Albert Embankment, London SE1 7TP
Website: www.wspa.org.uk

### World Wide Fund for Nature (WWF)
Panda House, Weyside Park, Godalming, Surrey GU7 1XR
Website: www.panda.org

## USA
### American Anti Vivisection Society
801 Old York Rd #204
Jenkintown, PA 19046-1685
Website: www.aavs.org

### American SPCA
424E 92nd Street, New York, NY 10128
Website: www.aspca.org

### American Humane Association
63 Inverness Drive East, Englewood, CO 80112-5117
Website: www.americanhumane.org

### The Humane Society of the United States
200 L Street NW, Washington DC 20037
Website: www.hsus.org

### International Fund for Animal Welfare
International HQ, 411 Main Street, PO Box 193, Yarmouth Port, MA 02675
Website: www.ifaw.org

### National Association for Biomedical Research
818 Conneticut Avenue NW, Suite 200, Washington DC 20006
Website: www.nabr.org

**People for the Ethical Treatment of Animals**
501 Front Street, Norfolk, VA 23510
Website: www.peta-online.org

AUSTRALIA
**Animal Rights Resource Centre**
PO Box 18, Kent Town,
S. Australia 5071
Website: www.arrc.org.au

**RSPCA Australia**
PO Box 265,
Deakin West, ACT 2600,
Australia
Website: www.rspca.org.au

NEW ZEALAND
**New Zealand Anti Vivisection Society**
PO Box 9387, Christchurch,
New Zealand
Website: www.nzavs.org.nz

**Royal New Zealand SPCA**
PO Box 15349, New Lynn,
Auckland 7,
New Zealand
Website: www.rspcanz.org.nz

## WEBSITES
**www.animalrights.net**
Despite the name, very anti the animal-rights movement. Go to FAQs for a long list of links to all sorts of information on people and issues worldwide.

**www.animal-rights.com**
Not to be confused with www.animalrights.net (see above). These people are for animal rights.

**www.cok.net**
US-based animal-rights group founded in the 1990s, Compassion over Killing campaigns for 'a kinder life for all'. Useful FAQ section on the thinking behind the animal-rights movement.

**www.kids4research.org**
How and why animals are used in research. Takes the view that animal experimentation may not be desirable – and one day may not be necessary at all – but that currently it's the only way of getting the information scientists need to develop drugs and other products that are safe for humans, animals and the environment.

# GLOSSARY

**abattoir** Place where animals are killed.

**Alzheimer's disease** Currently incurable brain illness, mainly affecting elderly people. The brain gradually loses its ability to function.

**amphibians** Animals like frogs, toads and newts that live both on land and in water.

**anaesthetics** Drugs given to eliminate the sensation of pain.

**animal welfare** Health and well-being of animals.

**antibiotic** Drug given to humans and animals to treat infections.

**asthma** Disease occurring in the lungs, causing breathing difficulties.

**blood transfusion** Injection of blood or blood products into a person or animal's vein. Used to replace blood lost during accident or injury.

**cloning** Scientific process used to create exact copies of cells, organs or whole animals.

**conservation** Protection and careful management of environmental and natural resources.

**cystic fibrosis** Inherited disease, usually affecting young children. Causes breathing difficulties and other symptoms.

**depression** Long-lasting feelings of deep sadness.

**diabetes** Condition caused by the body's inability to control the level of sugar in the blood.

**discrimination** Unfair treatment of person or group.

**domesticated animals** Wild animals brought or kept under human control.

**evolution** Gradual change over many years.

**exotic species** Animals not naturally living in a country, but brought into it by humans.

**exploitation** Situation where an animal or human is used for someone else's benefit.

**extinction** Death of an entire species.

**factory farming** Way of raising animals designed to increase the amount of meat, eggs or milk they produce.

**genes** Life-giving information transmitted from an organism to its offspring.

**habitat** The natural home of a particular living thing or group of living things.

**hormones** Chemicals produced by the body that are essential for growth or other function.

**humanely** With compassion, and inflicting the minimum of pain.

**intensive farming** Means of raising large numbers of animals on limited land (see factory farming).

**kidney dialysis** Medical procedure that takes over the job of filtering waste products from the body when someone's kidneys fail.

**livestock** Farm-reared animals.

**malaria** Potentially fatal disease carried to humans by some mosquitoes. Affects millions of people worldwide.

**monogastric species** Animal with a single stomach, like a chicken or pig.

**natural resource** Useful material produced by the Earth rather than humans.

**organ transplants** Operations that replace failing hearts, livers or kidneys with organs from another person.

**polluted** Contaminated with something harmful.

**ruminant species** Mammals such as sheep, goats, deer, camels and cattle that feed on plants.

**sentient** Able to think and feel.

**spinal-cord damage** Injury to nerves carrying information from the brain to the rest of the body, resulting in loss of movement.

**stroke** Sudden bursting of blood vessel in the brain, often leading to loss of movement or speech.

**Three Rs** Way of limiting numbers of animals used in research (reduction, refinement, replacement).

**vaccines** Medicines made from germs that cause disease, given to people to stop them getting it.

**vegans** People who choose not to eat or use anything that comes from animals.

**vegetarians** People who choose not to eat meat.

**xenotransplant** Transplant of animal organs into humans.

# INDEX

International Whaling
    Commission 43
Islam 22

Jews 22

King Jr, Martin Luther 6
Koko the gorilla 12
kosher meat 22

laboratory animals 45, 49
lambs 22
larks 15
leather 36, 37
lethal injection 16
Liberty and Livelihood
    March 41
lions 28, 51
livestock 6, 19, 24, 26, 48,
    55

malnutrition 24
McCartney, Sir Paul 42
meat 16, 18, 21
    chickens 18, 19
    consumption 19
    hormones 20, 24, 26, 54
    hunting 14
    prehistoric times 8
    supermarkets 25
media 27, 40, 41
medicines 34, 49
    traditional 17
mice 4, 35
Michael the gorilla 12
milk 8, 16, 20, 21, 48
mink 16
Muslims 22

organ transplants 34, 35,
    49, 55
organic farming 27, 38

pain 11, 12
panda conservation 47

parrots 12, 28
performing animals 29, 43
pesticides 27
pets 4, 28, 29, 30, 37, 38, 43
pigeon racing 30
pigs 19, 22, 23, 24, 34, 35, 48
ploughs 9
poachers 9
poultry 19, 27, 48
    slaughter 23
    stress 21
predators 14
prehistoric times 8
primates 9, 11, 28
product testing 5, 37

rabbits 4, 51
racoons 16
rats 12
religious leaders 10
religious slaughter 22
reptiles 28
rescue centres 5, 37, 38, 47
research 4, 32
RSPCA 38, 50, 52
Russell, W.M.S. 37

sadness 11, 12
safari parks 28
safaris 15
salmon 15, 20
Scandinavia 16
seals 16
sentient beings 13, 55
sheep 16, 17, 19, 55
    foot-and-mouth
    disease 24
    slaughter 22, 23
shellfish farms 20
Sikhism 22
Singer, Peter 7
skins 14, 15, 16, 39
    prehistoric times 8
slaughter 22–23, 27, 38
souvenirs 15

speciesism 7
sport 14, 15, 28, 30, 37, 39,
    45
starvation 24, 27, 44
stress 16, 21, 23
stunning 22, 23
supermarkets 25, 26, 27
survival of the fittest 9
swans 13

*The Origin of Species* 9
thrushes 12, 15
transport of animals 22
trapping 9, 14
travel 8
trophies 15
tuna 15, 16
tusks 15

UK 14, 15, 16, 19, 41, 43
United Nations 7
Universal Declaration of
    Human Rights 6, 7
USA,
    hunger 26
    hunting 15
    laws 43
    meat consumption 19

veal calves 20
vets 32
vitamins 18

whales 16, 43
wild animals 17, 38
    hunting 14, 15, 16
    research 34
wool 16, 17, 36
working animals 37
WSPA 43
WWF 47

xenotransplants 35, 55

zoos 28, 39